Meano Dino

Story by Sonja Smith
Pictures by Viango Studios

Permission should be addressed in writing to:
booktumes@gmail.com

Editor Wendy VanHatten
VanHatten Writing Services
www.wendyvanhatten.com

Cover design and Illustrations by Viango Studios
http://viangostudios.com

Layout by DocUmeant Designs
http://www.DocUmeantDesigns.com

ISBN13: 978-0-6927-6763-4
ISBN10: 0-692-76763-0

Dedication

To my loving mother, Vernita, who believes in all my endeavors.

For

My awesome, 2015-16 preschoolers, whose characters and ideas are present in this book.

Hi, I'm Princess Bailey and this is my classmate Meano Dino.
I want to be his friend, but sometimes he is grumpy and says hurtful things.

I am going to speak with him about his attitude. Perhaps he can choose kind words and stop being rude.

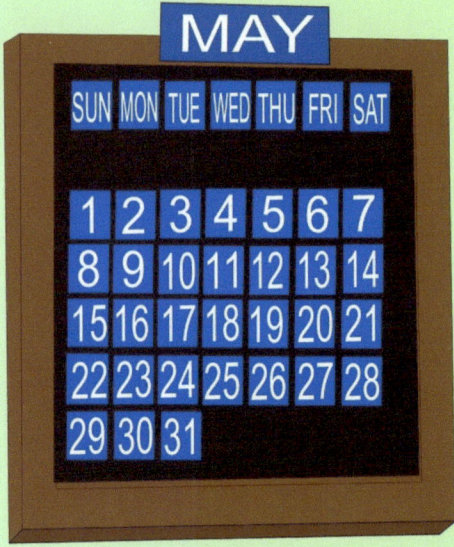

Meano Dino, what do you say,
will you be kind in the month of May?

I'm not your friend! I don't like you!

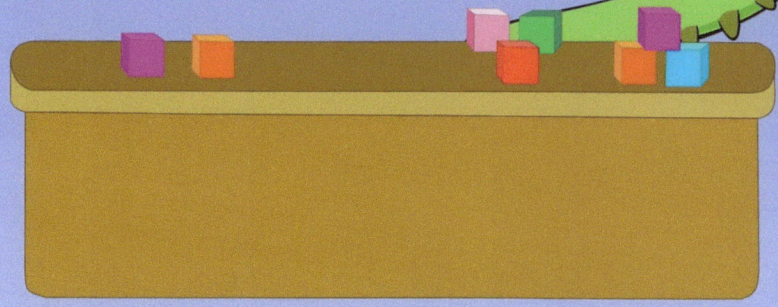

That hurt my feelings;
makes me feel sad.

Can you say something nice?
I bet you'll be glad!

I'm not going to play with you!
Gooooo awayyyyyyy!
Don't talk to me today!

If you continue to say hurtful, mean words, I will tell an adult; Mom, Dad, or teacher Ms. Byrd.

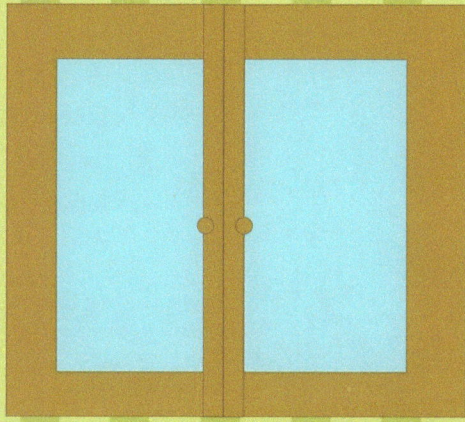

Oh NOOOOO!!

Pleasssssse don't tell that I'm being mean!
Sometimes I hear bad words
and like to repeat things.

Let's have a play date!
I will be your friend! We can share!
I love my family. School is fun!
Yes, please and thank you!

Words should be used to communicate ideas, express love and kindness. But neverrrrrr to make someone sad.

Meano Dino, what do you say,
will you be kind in the month of May?

Hmmmm...

I will! I will!
I am your friend!
Let's go play!

I feel happy when I say good things!
I do not wish to be grumpy and mean.
I will use words to express kindness every day.
Forever, much longer than the month of May!

Meano Dino you're a
Herrrrrrrro!

~School Readiness Tips~

Preparing your child for school has many facets. In this book, we focus on problem solving and social skills. Children will have the opportunity to enrich their vocabulary, hone their critical thinking skills and identify rhyming words. Costumes of the main characters will allow children to fully immerse themselves in the story while developing communication skills, imagination, self confidence and art appreciation.

Communication~ an integral skill to improve,because your child's ability to convey his or her own ideas and emotions is the core of all the fundamental learning skills.

Identifying Rhyming words~ can improve a child's speech, spelling skills and is crucial to pre-reading competencies.

Vocabulary~ is an essential part of literacy because it helps with comprehension.

Dramatic play~ allows children to experiment with roles of the people in their environment. It stimulates them to imagine situations and visualize solutions to different circumstances before they occur. Moreover, imagination is linked to your child's intellectual development.

Problem Solving/Critical Thinking skills~ are vital in promoting children to solve emerging problems, act with a rational mind and make sound judgements.

Social skills~ are also essential in a child's development. It fosters positive relationships with others and is key to school readiness and academic success.

~Vocabulary words to review~

Grumpy, hurtful, attitude, perhaps, choose, kind, rude, feelings, glad, continue, mean, repeat, communicate, express, hero.

~Critical thinking questions ~

What did Princess Bailey dislike about Meano Dino?
Why did Meano Dino say hurtful things?
What should Meano Dino say instead of hurtful words?
Why should you not say hurtful words to anyone?
What can you do if someone says hurtful words to you?

Author's Note

I wrote this book because as a preschool teacher, I wanted to design a fun and innovative way children could foster a genuine love of reading and learning. My aim was to enrich the children's pre reading skills, vocabulary and help them get the most out of books. This vision led me to create books with costumes for the main characters. Seventeen years of hands-on experience with children taught me they like to act out the role of a character in the story, and that the dramatic play area is one of the busiest places in the classroom. I envisioned this book to be an instrument that encourages children to love literature as much as motivates them to appreciate art in another form. Moreover, I wrote this book to develop and nurture their social skills, because that needs to be addressed for school readiness and its importance is something we cannot afford to overlook. Lastly, the 30 million word gap* steeled my resolve to make a difference, one reader at a time! The books I author will have a minimum of 9 vocabulary words to discuss with children. (It's been said if you teach a child 9 new vocabulary words per day you can bridge the gap* by the time the child reaches 3rd grade) Let's accomplish these goals together, this book, your child/children and you!

****The 30 Million Word Gap** -- a study conducted in the 90s revealed children from a higher socio-economic group know 30 million more words than a child from a lower socio-economic group by age **THREE.** (Hart and Risley, 1990)*

This book and costumes can be purchased at Amazon or booktumes.com

Acknowledgments

Thank you to everyone who helped
on this amazing journey!

To my children, Simone and Julian,
thanks for your suggestions and cheering
spirits during the making of this book.

Finally, thank you to my husband,
Rafael, who inspires me to do more! Your
motivation and support through this
process touched me dearly.